HARDSHIP
& SPIRITUAL
GROWTH

In the Words of 'Abdu'l-Bahá

BAHÁ'Í
PUBLISHING

WILMETTE, ILLINOIS

Bahá'í Publishing
401 Greenleaf Avenue, Wilmette, Illinois 60091
Copyright © 2021 by the National Spiritual Assembly
of the Bahá'ís of the United States
All rights reserved. Published 2021

Printed in the United States of America on acid-free paper ∞
24   23   22   21   4   3   2   1

ISBN 978-1-61851-199-7

Cover design by Carlos Esparza
Book design by Patrick Falso

Extracts 3–7, 9, 11, 13–16, 18, 19, 22, 24, 26, 28 are from *Selections from the Writings of 'Abdu'l-Bahá*. Wilmette, IL: Bahá'í Publishing, 2010.

Extract 21 is from *Some Answered Questions*. Haifa: Bahá'í World Centre, 2014.

Extracts 10, 27 are from *'Abdu'l-Bahá in London: Addresses and Notes of Conversations*. London: Bahá'í Publishing Trust, 1982.

Extracts 2, 12, 17, 23, 25 are from *Paris Talks: Addresses Given by 'Abdu'l-Bahá in Paris in 1911*. Wilmette, IL: Bahá'í Publishing, 2011.

Extracts 1, 8, 20 are from The *Promulgation of Universal Peace: Talks Delivered by 'Abdu'l-Bahá during His Visit to the United States and Canada in 1912*. Wilmette, IL: Bahá'í Publishing, 2012.

‘Abdu’l-Bahá

November 2021 will mark the hundredth anniversary of the passing of a figure beloved by many. ‘Abdu’l-Bahá, meaning *Servant of the Glory,* is the title assumed by Abbás Effendi (1844–1921), the son and appointed successor of Bahá’u’lláh—the Prophet and Founder of the Bahá’í Faith. ‘Abdu’l-Bahá shared a lifetime of exile with his Father at the hands of the Persian and Ottoman Empires, and was a prisoner for forty years. Despite the severe hardships that characterized his life, he dedicated his energy to the service of others and radiated joy and selfless contentment at all times. His charitable deeds and undiscriminating love for all are well documented in the accounts of countless souls who crossed his path, and his timeless and deep wisdom is recorded extensively in both his written works and in the transcripts of his many public addresses. He is known by Bahá’ís as the perfect exemplar of the Faith's teachings.

1

Even as Jesus Christ forfeited His life, may you, likewise, offer yourselves in the threshold of sacrifice for the betterment of the world; and just as Bahá'u'lláh suffered severe ordeals and calamities nearly fifty years for you, may you be willing to undergo difficulties and withstand catastrophes for humanity in general. May you bear these trials and tests most willingly and joyously, for every night is followed by a day, and every day has a night.

2

Tests are benefits from God, for which we should thank Him. Grief and sorrow do not come to us by chance, they are sent to us by the Divine Mercy for our own perfecting.

3

Rely upon God. Trust in Him. Praise Him, and call Him continually to mind. He verily turneth trouble into ease, and sorrow into solace, and toil into utter peace. He verily hath dominion over all things.

4

It is easy to approach the Kingdom of Heaven, but hard to stand firm and staunch within it, for the tests are rigorous, and heavy to bear.

5

Do not dwell on what is coming to pass . . . and be ye in no wise alarmed. Whatsoever may happen is for the best, because affliction is but the essence of bounty, and sorrow and toil are mercy unalloyed, and anguish is peace of mind, and to make a sacrifice is to receive a gift, and whatsoever may come to pass hath issued from God's grace.

6

O thou who art turning thy face towards God! Close thine eyes to all things else, and open them to the realm of the All-Glorious. Ask whatsoever thou wishest of Him alone; seek whatsoever thou seekest from Him alone. With a look He granteth a hundred thousand hopes, with a glance He healeth a hundred thousand incurable ills, with a nod He layeth balm on every wound, with a glimpse He freeth the hearts from the shackles of grief. He doeth as He doeth, and what recourse have we? He carrieth out His Will, He ordaineth what He pleaseth. Then better for thee to bow down thy head in submission, and put thy trust in the All-Merciful Lord.

7

My only joy in this swiftly passing world was to tread the stony path of God and to endure hard tests and all material griefs. For otherwise, this earthly life would prove barren and vain, and better would be death. The tree of being would produce no fruit; the sown field of this existence would yield no harvest. Thus it is my hope that once again some circumstance will make my cup of anguish to brim over, and that beauteous Love, that Slayer of souls, will dazzle the beholders again. Then will this heart be blissful, this soul be blessed.

8

O Lord! Verily, we are weak; make us mighty. We are poor; assist us from the treasury of Thy munificence. We are dead; resuscitate us through the breath of the Holy Spirit. We lack patience in tests and in long-suffering; permit us to attain the lights of oneness.

9

O sincere servant of the True One! I hear thou art grieved and distressed at the happenings of the world and the vicissitudes of fortune. Wherefore this fear and sorrow? The true lovers of the Abhá Beauty, and they that have quaffed the Cup of the Covenant fear no calamity, nor feel depressed in the hour of trial. They regard the fire of adversity as their garden of delight, and the depth of the sea the expanse of heaven.

10

. . . Bahá'u'lláh underwent great difficulties and hardships. He was in constant confinement and He suffered great persecution. But in the fortress ('Akká) He reared a spiritual palace and from the darkness of His prison He sent out a great light to the world.

11

When calamity striketh, be ye patient and composed. However afflictive your sufferings may be, stay ye undisturbed, and with perfect confidence in the abounding grace of God, brave ye the tempest of tribulations and fiery ordeals.

12

If sorrow and adversity visit us, let us turn our faces to the Kingdom and heavenly consolation will be outpoured.

13

Prosperity, contentment, and freedom, however much desired and conducive to the gladness of the human heart, can in no wise compare with the trials of homelessness and adversity in the pathway of God; for such exile and banishment are blessed by the divine favor, and are surely followed by the mercy of Providence.

14

The tests of every dispensation are in direct proportion to the greatness of the Cause, and as heretofore such a manifest Covenant, written by the Supreme Pen, hath not been entered upon, the tests are proportionately more severe. These trials cause the feeble souls to waver while those who are firm are not affected. These agitations of the violators are no more than the foam of the ocean, which is one of its inseparable features; but the ocean of the Covenant shall surge and shall cast ashore the bodies of the dead, for it cannot retain them.

15

While the children are yet in their infancy feed them from the breast of heavenly grace, foster them in the cradle of all excellence, rear them in the embrace of bounty. Give them the advantage of every useful kind of knowledge. Let them share in every new and rare and wondrous craft and art. Bring them up to work and strive, and accustom them to hardship. Teach them to dedicate their lives to matters of great import, and inspire them to undertake studies that will benefit mankind.

16

To the loyal soul, a test is but God's grace and favor; for the valiant doth joyously press forward to furious battle on the field of anguish, when the coward, whimpering with fright, will tremble and shake. . . .

It is clear, then, that tests and trials are, for sanctified souls, but God's bounty and grace, while to the weak, they are a calamity, unexpected and sudden.

These tests . . . do but cleanse the spotting of self from off the mirror of the heart, till the Sun of Truth can cast its rays thereon; for there is no veil more obstructive than the self, and however tenuous that veil may be, at the last it will completely shut a person out, and deprive him of his portion of eternal grace.

17

While a man is happy he may forget his God; but when grief comes and sorrows overwhelm him, then will he remember his Father who is in Heaven, and who is able to deliver him from his humiliations.

Men who suffer not, attain no perfection. The plant most pruned by the gardeners is that one which, when the summer comes, will have the most beautiful blossoms and the most abundant fruit.

18

If the Manifestations are subjected to tests, it is in Their human station only, not in the splendor of Their Divine Reality.

And further, these tests are such only from the viewpoint of mankind. That is, to outward seeming, the human condition of the Holy Manifestations is subjected to tests, and when Their strength and endurance have by this means been revealed in the plenitude of power, other men receive instruction therefrom, and are made aware of how great must be their own steadfastness and endurance under tests and trials. For the Divine Educator must teach by word and also by deed, thus revealing to all the straight pathway of truth.

19

. . . the tests and trials of God take place in this world, not in the world of the Kingdom.

20

. . . the poor are especially beloved of God. Their lives are full of difficulties, their trials continual, their hopes are in God alone. Therefore, you must assist the poor as much as possible, even by sacrifice of yourself. No deed of man is greater before God than helping the poor. Spiritual conditions are not dependent upon the possession of worldly treasures or the absence of them. When one is physically destitute, spiritual thoughts are more likely. Poverty is a stimulus toward God. Each one of you must have great consideration for the poor and render them assistance. Organize in an effort to help them and prevent increase of poverty. The greatest means for prevention is that whereby the laws of the community will be so framed and enacted that it will not be possible for a few to be millionaires and many destitute.

21

Now, the root cause of these difficulties lies in the law of nature that governs present-day civilization, for it results in a handful of people accumulating vast fortunes that far exceed their needs, while the greater number remain naked, destitute, and helpless. This is at once contrary to justice, to humanity, and to fairness; it is the very height of inequity and runs counter to the good-pleasure of the All-Merciful.

. . . there is neither equality here nor benevolence. Observe how, as a result, general peace and happiness have become so wanting, and the welfare of humanity so undermined, that the lives of a vast multitude have been rendered fruitless! For all the wealth, power, commerce, and industry are concentrated in the hands of a few individuals, while all others toil under the burden of endless hardships and difficulties, are bereft of advantages and benefits, and remain deprived of comfort and peace. One must therefore enact such laws and regulations as will moderate the excessive fortunes of the few and meet the basic needs of the myriad millions of the poor, that a degree of moderation may be achieved.

22

Gracious God! How strange that, notwithstanding these conclusive proofs, every day some event transpireth and difficulties arise. But we, and the friends of God, should on no account slacken our efforts to be loyal, sincere and . . . of good will. We should at all times manifest our truthfulness and sincerity, nay rather, we must be constant in our faithfulness and trustworthiness, and occupy ourselves in offering prayers for the good of all.

23

The mind and spirit of man advance when he is tried by suffering. The more the ground is ploughed the better the seed will grow, the better the harvest will be. Just as the plough furrows the earth deeply, purifying it of weeds and thistles, so suffering and tribulation free man from the petty affairs of this worldly life until he arrives at a state of complete detachment. His attitude in this world will be that of divine happiness. Man is, so to speak, unripe: the heat of the fire of suffering will mature him. Look back to the times past and you will find that the greatest men have suffered most.

24

Do not grieve at the afflictions and calamities that have befallen thee. All calamities and afflictions have been created for man so that he may spurn this mortal world—a world to which he is much attached. When he experienceth severe trials and hardships, then his nature will recoil and he will desire the eternal realm—a realm which is sanctified from all afflictions and calamities. Such is the case with the man who is wise.

25

Consider the great sorrows endured by Christ and by His apostles!

Those who suffer most, attain to the greatest perfection.

Those who declare a wish to suffer much for Christ's sake must prove their sincerity; those who proclaim their longing to make great sacrifices can only prove their truth by their deeds.

26

. . . when exalting the Word of God, there are trials to be met with, and calamities; and that in loving Him, at every moment there are hardships, torments, afflictions.

It behooveth the individual first to value these ordeals, willingly accept them, and eagerly welcome them; only then should he proceed with teaching the Faith and exalting the Word of God.

In such a state, no matter what may befall him in his love for God—harassment, reproach, vilification, curses, beatings, imprisonment, death—he will never be cast down, and his passion for the Divine Beauty will but gain in strength.

27

Freedom is not a matter of place. It is a condition. I was thankful for the prison, and the lack of liberty was very pleasing to me, for those days were passed in the path of service, under the utmost difficulties and trials, bearing fruits and results.

Unless one accepts dire vicissitudes, he will not attain. To me prison is freedom, troubles rest me, death is life, and to be despised is honour. Therefore, I was happy all that time in prison. When one is released from the prison of self, that is indeed release, for that is the greater prison. When this release takes place, then one cannot be outwardly imprisoned. When they put my feet in stocks, I would say to the guard, "You cannot imprison me, for here I have light and air and bread and water. There will come a time when my body will be in the ground, and I shall have neither light nor air nor food nor water, but even then I shall not be imprisoned." The afflictions which come to humanity sometimes tend to centre the consciousness upon the limitations, and this is a veritable prison. Release comes by making of the will a Door through which the confirmations of the Spirit come.

28

The beloved of the Lord must stand fixed as the mountains, firm as impregnable walls. Unmoved must they remain by even the direst adversities, ungrieved by the worst of disasters. Let them cling to the hem of Almighty God, and put their faith in the Beauty of the Most High; let them lean on the unfailing help that cometh from the Ancient Kingdom, and depend on the care and protection of the generous Lord.